Monumental New Orleans

History in Stone

Kathy Chappetta Spiess

Beautiful Crescent
Books

Monumental New Orleans
Copyright © 2017 by Kathleen Chappetta Spiess

ISBN: 978-0692950364

Dedication

For the brave men and women who serve in our military, protecting the United States and ensuring that we enjoy the freedoms granted by the United States Constitution.

Books edited by Kathy Chappetta Spiess

Beautiful Crescent – A History of New Orleans
(by Widmer & Garvey)

Louisiana First 300 Years
(by Widmer & Garvey)

Table of Contents

Author's Note

The idea of this book came to me a couple of years ago while studying to become a Professional Tour Guide. The sheer number of monuments in the city staggered me, but what surprised me even more was the number of monuments I knew nothing about. Right then I decided to write this book.

While putting this book together, I tried to capture all the major statues, monuments and memorials that grace the streets and parks of New Orleans. I'm sure that I've missed a few, but feel that I've included most of them here in this book. If I have missed any memorial or monument it was not intentional.

I hope you enjoy reading *Monumental New Orleans*. In it you will discover some of the people and events that helped to make New Orleans the unique and culturally rich city that it is today.

Introduction

Monuments are everywhere. They can be in the form of a statue, building, plaque or pillar. They are erected in memory and/or to honor a person or event.

Recently, certain monuments have been the target of, for lack of a better word, terrorists. A group of people who vandalize and destroy what *they* find offensive. While their arguments may be, and often are, valid. Their violent actions and destruction nullify any message they may have. Our right to free speech gives every person, group and government, the right to give voice to their opinions and beliefs. It gives us the right to worship as we please and, yes, to put up monuments to people and events we value. Free speech also gives these "anti" groups the right to protest those same monuments we value. It does not, however, give them the right to damage and destroy property or people.

Before we vilify any monument, we should understand that monuments say more about the people who erected them and the governments that allowed them to be erected on public ground, than the subject of the monument. These memorials reflect the times and emotions of the times they were erected. Remembrances of wars won and the brave who fought in them and to mourn their loss or what could have been. People are honored to show appreciation for what they've done and who they were. But no man, woman or event is without flaws. Look hard enough and you will see something distasteful or offensive in everyone and everything. But the baby shouldn't be thrown out with the bathwater. Yes, George Washington owned slaves, as did a good number of people of his day, but his bravery in leading the United States toward independence is why we honor him with more than 300 statues throughout the United States, not counting the bridges, buildings and roads named after him.

Monuments are milestones that mark the evolution of civilization. They all teach something – some teach goals and ideals to strive for and hold dear, like freedom and sacrifice, civic duty and philanthropy. Others teach us things we should not forget lest we repeat the mistakes of the past such as slavery and exploitation, ignorance and intolerance. Isn't that what we want to teach our children? To emulate and value the things that make us grow and evolve as human beings, and avoid those things that don't.

The history doesn't go away because someone disagrees with the method of remembrance and decides to remove or destroy the symbol. Wouldn't time and money be better spent finding ways to promote a complete understanding rather than violence and eradication?

French Quarter

Jean Baptiste Le Moyne

Jean Baptiste LeMoyne, Sieur de Bienville
Decatur Street, north of Conti Street
Erected: 1955

In 1699, Jean Baptiste LeMoyne, Sieur de Bienville, accompanied his brother Pierre LeMoyne d'Iberville, on an expedition from France to find the mouth of the Mississippi River.

The brothers found the Mississippi and claimed all the land drained by the great river for France and people began to settle in the new colony.

In 1717, Bienville found a crescent in the river, safe from tidal surges and hurricanes on which to build the capitol of the colony. This is where he built Nouvelle Orléans.

The Louisiana Purchase Sesquicentennial Committee originally erected this statue of Bienville at Bienville Plaza, which at the time, was located near the New Orleans Union Train station in April 1955. It was relocated to Bienville Place on Decatur St. in November 1996.

The statue, created by Angela Gregory, depicts Bienville standing straight and tall; at his back is Father Athanese and seated is a Native American with peace pipe.

Monument Plaque:
Jean Baptiste LeMoyne, de Bienville born Montreal, February 23, 1680, died March 7, 1767. Founder of New Orleans 1717. With homage of Louisiana – Canada – France.

3

Andrew Jackson
Jackson Square/Place d'Armes
Erected: 1851

General Andrew Jackson is celebrated in New Orleans and his statue stands in Jackson Square in front of the St. Louis Cathedral.

The statue of Andrew Jackson was erected in 1856 by the Jackson Monument Association. The statue is one of four equestrian statues of him created by Clark Mills. The other three statues can be found in Washington, DC (1853), Nashville, TN (1880) and Jacksonville, FL (1987).

Today, Andrew Jackson is a controversial figure. He owned up to 300 slaves in his lifetime and was instrumental in the federal government forcibly removing American Indians from native lands, resulting in the "Trail of Tears." While these facts have tarnished Jackson's historical image, they are not what is celebrated in New Orleans. The statue of Andrew Jackson so prominently displayed in the Jackson Square, celebrates his victory at the Battle of New Orleans in which he led a militia against the British, winning the final battle of the War of 1812.

Jackson Square Fountain
Erected: 1960

The water fountain in Jackson Square, standing between Andrew Jackson's statue and the St. Louis Cathedral was erected to commemorate the visit of Charles de Gaulle, President of France, to New Orleans in 1960.

5

Photo credit: 4kclips/shutterstock.com

Joan of Arc, *LaPucelle d'Orleans* (Maid of Orleans)
Decatur Street @ St. Philip St., near the French Market
Erected: 1972

History reports that Joan of Arc received visions of the Archangel Michael, St. Margaret and St. Catherine of Alexandria telling her to fight in support of Charles VIII to recover France from the English.

In carrying out this mission, the brave Joan was captured on May 30, 1430 by the Buyandian faction, allies of England. She was put on trial and found guilty. She was burned at the stake in Rouen at 19 years of age.

In 1452, Joan's mother, Isabella Romée, and Inquisitor General Jean Bréhal requested that Joan be retried, posthumously. Pope Callixtus III authorized the "nullification trial" and the charges were debunked. She was pronounced innocent and declared a martyr on July 7, 1456.

The statue of Joan of Arc in New Orleans was a gift to the city from the people of France. It is an exact replica of the equestrian statue commissioned by Napoleon III in 1874 and sculpted by Emmanuel Frémiet.

Originally, the statue of Joan of Arc was erected in 1972 in front of the International Trade Mart Building. Construction of the land based casino forced the city to relocate the statue to its present location at "Place De France" on Decatur St. at the corner of St. Philip St., near the French Market in the French Quarter. Joan is depicted with two canons and she rides into New Orleans on horseback with banners held high. The statue, originally a golden bronze, was gilded in 1985.

A second statue of St. Joan of Arc (right) can be found in the St. Louis Cathedral on Jackson Square. This statue, donated to the Cathedral by "The Sodality of Saint Joan of Arc" in 1920, is inscribed: *"Donnés par sodazité de Ste. Jeanne D' Arc 1920."*

King Louis IX of France/St. Louis
615 Pere Antoine Alley

If you go half way down Pere Antoine Alley, between the St. Louis Cathedral and the Presbytere, and look up you'll find the statue of Louis IX, sainted King of France.

Crowned at the age of 12 in Reims, Louis IX performed many charitable acts and was devout in his religious practices. He was widely considered a fair and just monarch. While he was known to be quick tempered and sometimes violent, he was devoted to the arts and literature and in "freeing the Holy Land" from Islam. Louis participated in the 7th and 8th crusades in 1248 and 1267, respectively.

King Louis IX died during the 8th crusade, in Tunisia. After his death, crowds gathered along the roadsides and knelt as his body passed by on its way to France for burial.

Pope Boniface VIII canonized Louis IX, King of France on August 9, 1297, after the church examined 65 miracles attesting to his sanctity.

Prayer to St. Louis, Feast Day August 25:

> *"O God, who called your servant Louis of France to an earthly throne
> that he might advance your heavenly kingdom, and
> gave him zeal for your Church and love for your people:
> Mercifully grant that we who commemorate him this day be fruitful in
> good works, and attain to the glorious crown of your saints;
> through Jesus Christ our Lord, who lives and reigns with you
> and the Holy Spirit, one God for ever and ever."*

Henriette Delille – Servant of the Slaves
Royal Street, Behind St. Louis Cathedral

The Venerable Henriette Delille was an American-born Free Person of Color. A devout woman, she dedicated herself to caring for the poor and sick of New Orleans, most of whom were slaves.

At the age of 24, Henriette drew up rules and regulations for devout Christian women. This would eventually become the tenets of the Sisters of the Holy Family. Henriette, along with two friends, Juliette Gaudin and Josephine Charles, set up a three-part approach to their program: they expressed their apostolic intentions through caring for the sick, helping the poor and instructing the ignorant of their people, enslaved and free children and adults, in the name of Jesus Christ and the Church.

These three young women took in elderly people and established the first Catholic home for the elderly (recorded in the National Register).

In her quest to live a devout life, she bore many crosses, encountered many obstacles and suffered personal illness. Henriette Delille faced resistance to her idea of a black religious order, suffered from lack of funds to perform her mission and had no support from the Catholic Church. She succeeded in her mission through tremendous perseverance.

The Sisters of the Holy Family have worked tirelessly in their efforts to have Henriette declared a saint. Canonization is a four-step process in the Catholic Church: servant of God, Venerable, Blessed and Saint.

With the help of the late Archbishop Philip Hannon, Pope John Paul II declared Henriette a Servant of God in 1988. Pope Benedict XVI declared her Venerable in 2010. The remaining step is the validation of an alleged miracle, which is now under way.

Henriette Delille is the first native-born, African American to be considered for sainthood by the Catholic Church.

Sr. Delille statue in the old Ursuline Convent garden in the French Quarter.

Sr. Delille stained glass in St .Louis Cathedral

St. Louis Cathedral
Jackson Square
Established 1718

The St. Louis Cathedral, the third structure to sit on the site designated by Bienville in 1718, is a testament to the city's Catholic heritage.

Riverfront

Mother River
Port of New Orleans

At the Port of New Orleans stands Mother River (left), a graceful sculpture by Joseph Cleary. It represents the power, beauty and history of the Mississippi River that stretches from the Gulf of Mexico to the Canadian border.

Ocean Song
Woldenberg Park/Riverfront

On the banks of the Mississippi River stands Ocean Song, a stainless-steel sculpture by local artist John Scott. The sculpture, which honors the river that gave life to the city, depicts the motion of water in eight narrow pyramids.

Monument to the Immigrants
Woldenberg Park/Riverfront

New Orleans is a city built by immigrants. French, West Indians, Africans, and Spanish, are only a few of the nationalities that made New Orleans the culturally rich city it is today. On the Mississippi riverfront is a statue of white Carrera marble honoring the people that invested their hopes and dreams in the city. Created by Franco Allesandrine, the statue features a ship's prow topped by a female figure facing the river. Behind her, facing the French Quarter stands a turn of the century immigrant family.

Old Man River
Woldenberg Park/Riverfront

Another statue inspired by the Mississippi River is the 18-foot stone man. This sculpture is made of Carrera marble. It was sculpted by Robert Schoen and it speaks to the river's power and life force.

16

Holocaust Memorial
Woldenberg Park/Riverfront

Israeli artist and sculptor, Jacob (Yaacov) Agam, created the Holocaust Memorial. It is considered a "living work." As you walk around the nine colorful panels, the image changes. The memorial was created and erected in memory of the six million Jews and Jewish collaborators tortured and killed by the Nazis 1933-1945. The monument was dedicated in 2003.

General P.G.T. Beauregard

Civil War

P.G.T. Beauregard
City Park Ave. and Wisner Blvd.
Erected: 1915, Removed: 2017

Pierre Gustave Toutant-Beauregard was born at "Contreras" sugar plantation in St. Bernard Parish. He was a French Creole military officer who served with distinction in the Mexican American War.

When the southern states succeeded from the Union in 1861, Beauregard resigned his commission with the U.S. Army and became the first brigadier general of the Confederate army. Beauregard commanded the defenses of Charleston, SC at Fort Sumter.

After the South lost the war, Beauregard swore the oath of loyalty to the Union and was pardoned by President Andrew Johnson.

After the Civil War, Beauregard, a Democrat, worked to end the Republicans' role during Reconstruction. He was active in the reform party and spoke in favor of civil rights and giving the recently freed slaves the right to vote.

Beauregard died in New Orleans on February 20, 1893. He was the last surviving high-level Confederate military leader. His remains are interred in the vault of the Army of Tennessee in Metairie Cemetery.

After his death, the Beauregard Monument Association was formed and began appeals for donations to erect a monument to P.G.T. Beauregard saying that it would be "an enduring expression of his soldiers and countrymen's admiration." It wasn't until 1908 that Alexander Doyle was hired to create the statue. The City Park Association donated a plot of land at the entrance to the park for the monument. It would be another five years before the cornerstone for the monument was laid in a large ceremony on November 11, 1915.

A little more than 100 years later in 2017, Mayor Mitch Landrieu and the City Council had the statue removed.

Charles Didier Dreux
Jefferson Davis Parkway
Erected: Early 1920s

Charles Didier Dreux was the first soldier to answer the Confederate "call to arms" and one of the first to die during the war. Dreux came from a prominent New Orleans Creole family and served as a district attorney and member of the state legislature before the war. He is buried in the Army of Tennessee, Louisiana Division Memorial vault in Metairie Cemetery.

The statue of Dreux stands on Jefferson Davis Parkway and was dedicated on the 61st anniversary of his departure for the war. The statue was created by Victor Holm and the pedestal was designed by Albert Weiblen.

Monument reads:
Col. Charles Didier Dreux. Born in New Orleans May 11, 1832. First Confederate officer from Louisiana killed in the war between the states on the field of honor near Newport News, Virginia on July 5, 1861. His last words were "Boys. Steady." Nobler Braver Never Lived.

Fr. Abram J. Ryan
S. Jefferson Davis Parkway
Erected: 1949

Called the "Poet Priest" of the Confederacy, Fr. Abram J. Ryan was the unofficial chaplain of Confederate troops. His most famous poem is engraved on his monument.

Father Abram J. Ryan.
Poet Priest of the Confederacy. 1834-1886
Furl the banner for 'tis weary;
Round its staff 'tis drooping dreary;
Furl it, fold it – Let it rest!
Erected by Louisiana Division United
Daughters of the Confederacy 1949.

Albert Pike
S. Jefferson Davis Pkwy
Erected: 1957

General Albert Pike was a
Confederate officer assigned to
the Department of the Indian
Territory. He resigned his commission in 1862 when he and his
regiment were charged with
scalping northern soldiers.

When he died in April 1891, he
was a high-ranking Freemason.

Statue inscription:

*General Albert Pike, Confederate
States Army 1809-1891. Soldier,
Philosopher, Scholar. Grand Com-
mander Supreme Council 33º
Ancient & Accepted Scottish Rite
of Freemasonry Southern Juris-
diction USA 1859-1891.*

[Statue] *Erected April 27, 1959 by the Grand Consistory of LA, 32 º Ancient and
Accepted Rite of Freemasonry to commemorate the session of the Supreme Council
33 º A.A.S.R. held in New Orleans on April 25, 1857 when General Albert Pike
was coroneted at 33 º Mason and Inspector General Honorary.*

23

Jefferson Davis
South Jefferson Davis Pkwy
Erected: 1911, Removed 2017

A U.S. Senator before the Civil War, Jefferson Davis argued against succession. However, when the state of Mississippi seceded in 1861, he resigned from the senate, showing allegiance to his home state.

Davis was appointed Major General of the Army of Mississippi and later, was elected president of the newly formed Confederate States of America.

He was captured at the end of the war on May 10 and was imprisoned at Fortress Monroe in the Virginia under the authority of General Nelson Miles. While there he was shackled and allowed no visitors and no books except the Bible. He was released after two years. At the end of 1868, he received a pardon from President Andrew Johnson.

Liberty Place Monument
Erected: 1891, Removed: 2017

Probably the most controversial monument ever erected in New Orleans is the one memorializing the Battle of Liberty Place.

Reconstruction was a trying time for most southern cities. It lasted for a decade after Lee's surrender in April 1865. During Reconstruction, southern political power was in the hands of northern carpetbaggers and a few southern whites.

In September 1874, a few thousand men from the Crescent City White League met on Canal Street to face off with black policemen and the state militia to take control of the government after a contested gubernatorial election. Order was restored in the city only after Federal troops arrived.

The Liberty Place monument was erected by the New Orleans city government in 1891 on the neutral ground near the foot of Canal Street. In 1932, the city added an inscription to the monument attesting to the battle's role in "establishing white supremacy."

By late in the 20th century, the Liberty Monument was the scene and topic of much dissention and protest. In 1981, Mayor Dutch Morial called for its removal saying it *"has long been a source of divisiveness in our community."* Eventually the City Council relocated the monument to a less prominent location – one block off Canal St. at the end of Iberville, between a parking garage and floodwall.

After the 2015 shooting at a church in Charleston, South Carolina, many southern states began to rethink the public display of Confederate symbols and monuments. Mayor Mitch Landrieu and the City Council called for the Liberty Monument and three other confederate monuments (Lee, Beauregard and Davis) be removed.

On the night of April 24, 2017, the monument was removed by workers in bullet proof vests, protected by police snipers.

Photo credit: Eric Van Overton/shutterstock.com

Robert E. Lee
Lee Circle
Erected: 1884, Removed: 2017

General Robert E. Lee, former Superintendent of the Military at West Point, is best known for his role as general in the army of the Confederate States of America. Lee, who distinguished himself in the Mexican War, gave up his appointment at West Point to join his home state of Virginia when it succeeded from the Union in 1861. He surrendered to Union general, Ulysses S. Grant, at Appomattox Court House on April 9, 1865.

After the war, Lee openly opposed slavery and supported President Johnson's plan for Reconstruction, but he opposed the radical Republican demand for punitive measures against the South.

Today, historians suggest that Lee's public opposition to slavery after the war helped him maintain his stature as a symbol of southern honor and national reconciliation.

Alexander Doyle created the Robert E. Lee statue; architect John Ray designed the base and pedestal. It was installed at what was then Tivoli Circle (now Lee Circle) in 1884. The 16 ½ foot statue sat atop a column of white marble until 2017 when Mayor Landrieu and the City Council ordered it removed.

Metairie Cemetery

Metairie Cemetery is a historic cemetery that opened in 1868. The cemetery has many funereal monuments for individuals and groups, including four monuments dedicated to men who fought in the Civil War.

Benevolent Association,
Army of Tennessee, Louisiana Division
Metairie Cemetery
Erected: 1887

On the edge of Metairie Cemetery, near the corner of the Pontchartrain Expressway and City Park Avenue stands the tumulus of the Army of Tennessee (left).

A *tumulus* is an artificial mound of earth raised over a grave. The tumulus in Metairie Cemetery, designed by famed tomb contractor, Pierre Casse, was built by the Army of Tennessee Benevolent Society.

Atop the tumulus stands the equestrian statue of General Albert Sidney Johnston and near the entrance to the vault stands a life-sized statue of a soldier. The vault contains 48 crypts. Among the dead buried in the tumulus are Charles Didier Dreux, Lt. General Richard "Dick" Taylor (son of President Zachary Taylor), P.G.T. Beauregard, and John Dimitry.

General Albert Sidney Johnston
Metairie Cemetery
Erected: 1887

A statue of an officer on horseback stands on top of the tumulus of the Army of Tennessee, Louisiana Division. It is of Confederate General Albert S. Johnston. Johnston, astride his horse arm, raised as if directing his troops. The bronze monument was unveiled in 1887, 20 years after the end of the Civil War.

Designed by Alexander Doyle, it is an imposing statue of the general leading a charge.

While he is not buried in the tumulus, General Albert Sidney Johnston's lengthy epitaph is included on a plaque at the back of the vault.

"Albert Sidney Johnston. A General in the Army of the Confederate States, who fell at Shiloh, Tennessee, on the sixth day of April Eighteen Hundred and Sixty-two. A man tried in many high offices and critical enterprises and found faithful in all. His life was one long sacrifice of interest to conscience and even that life, on a woeful Sabbath, did he yield as a Holocaust at his country's need. Not wholly understood was he while he lived; but in his death, his greatness stands confessed in a People's tears. Resolute, moderate, clear of envy, yet not wanting in that finer ambition that makes men great and pure, in his honor – impregnable; in his simplicity – sublime. No country e'er had a truer son, no cause a nobler champion, no people a bolder defender, No principal a purer victim than the dead soldier! His fame consigned to the keeping of that time which, happily Is not so much the tomb of Virtue as its Shrine, shall in the years to come fire Modest Worth to Noble Ends. In honor now our great Captain rests; a bereaved people mourn him; three commonwealths proudly claim him; and history shall cherish him; among those choice spirits, who holding their conscience unmixed with blame, have been in all Conjunctures true to themselves, their People and their God.

Every Soldier
Metairie Cemetery
Erected: 1887

The life-sized statue of a soldier that stands near the vault entrance, also designed by Doyle, is of a Confederate soldier reading the roll of the dead. This statue represents "every soldier."

It is said that the statue was modeled after Sgt. William Brunet of the Louisiana Guard Battery. When originally sculpted, a rifle was placed in the crook of the soldier's arm, but was stolen. A second rifle was placed on the statue, anchored with a dowel,

30

theoretically to prevent theft. That one, too, was stolen. The thief, however, would not recoup any reward for his daring as he dropped the rifle as he jumped the fence and it broke. It was not replaced.

Army of Northern Virginia
Metairie Cemetery
Erected: 1881

Also in Metairie Cemetery is the tumulus for the Army of Northern Virginia Monument, established in 1881. On top of this tumulus is a 38-foot pillar on which stands the granite statue of General Thomas "Stonewall" Jackson, designed by Achille Perelli. But, like General Johnston of the Army of Tennessee, General Thomas Jackson is buried elsewhere. Inside the vault of the monument are 57 crypts in which 2500 men are buried.

The monument honors the Army of Northern Virginia, which was the primary Confederate force operating between the Appalachian Mountains and the Mississippi River.

Washington Artillery
Metairie Cemetery
Erected: 1880

The monument to the Louisiana's Washington Artillery can be found at the intersection of Avenues D and I in Metairie Cemetery. This monument is a memorial centograph – a monument without burials.

31

The Washington Artillery monument, designed by Charles A. Orleans and sculpted by George Doyle, consists of a 32-foot granite pillar on which stands an artillery soldier leaning on a gun swab. Surrounding the mound are upright cannon-shaped posts connected with iron chains.

Confederate Tumulus
Greenwood Cemetery, City Park Avenue
Erected: 1874

The tall shaft of another Confederate monument rises from a granite foundation and sits atop a tumulus in Greenwood Cemetery. At the base of the shaft are the faces of the Confederacy, General Thomas "Stonewall" Jackson, General Albert Sidney Johnston, General Leonidas Polk and General R. E. Lee.

A life-sized statue of a soldier of the Confederacy stands in uniform on top of the shaft, standing guard, in an easy attitude, leaning on his gun. The monument is made of Carrara marble and was designed by B. M. Harrod.

Lamp Post Medallions
Canal Street and Rampart Street

A Confederate medallion (right) graces one side of the base of the lamp posts that line Canal and Rampart Streets.

The lamp posts, a gift to New Orleans from France, are replicas of the lamps that line the *Champs Élysée*. There are four medallions around the base of the posts, each representing a government that ruled New Orleans throughout its history.

French Dominion – 1699-1769
Spanish Dominion – 1769-1803
United States Dominion – 1803-1861 & 1865- present
Confederate States Dominion – 1861-1865

Louisiana Civil War Museum
Confederate Memorial Hall
929 Camp Street.

The Louisiana Civil War Museum was built in the Richardsonian Romanesque style of Henry Hudson Richardson by Sully and Toledano Architects. It contains the largest collection of Confederate artifacts.

The National World War II Museum
945 Magazine Street
Established: 2000

The WWII Museum is located in the Central Business District. It tells the story of how the "war that changed the world" affected the United States and its people. It is a tribute to the men and women who served.

Military and War

Chalmette Battlefield
Battle of New Orleans.
8606 W. St. Bernard Highway, Chalmette, LA

The Battle of New Orleans was the last major battle in the War of 1812.

On January 8, 1815, under the leadership of General Andrew Jackson, a force comprised of army regulars, militiamen, frontiersmen, free blacks, Indians and even New Orleans aristocrats faced the British army under the leadership of Lt. General Sir Edward Pakenham at a field in what is now St. Bernard Parish.

Unbeknownst to Packenham as he prepared to attack Louisiana, the British and the Americans were meeting in Ghent, Belgium, to discuss terms to end the war. The Treaty of Ghent was signed on December 24. Britain ratified the treaty on December 30, 1814, but notice of the treaty did not reach Packenham before the Battle of New Orleans. The U.S. ratified the treaty on February 6, 1815, five weeks after the Battle of New Orleans.

In the battle that lasted about 30 minutes, Jackson and the Americans lost less than 100 men. The British lost 2,000 men and their last hope to ever win back their New World colonies.

President James Monroe remarked, "*History records no example of so glorious a victory obtained with so little bloodshed on the part of the victors.*" Addressing his troops, Jackson said, "*Natives of different states, acting together for the first time in this camp have reaped the fruits of an honorable union.*"

The site of the Battle of New Orleans is now a part of the National Park Service. A monument honoring the troops that fought at the Battle of New

Orleans stands on the grounds of the battlefield. It is 100-feet high with 122 interior steps leading to a viewing platform.

Was it military genius or Divine Intervention?

Packenham arrived in Louisiana ready to invade New Orleans and determined to take control of the river. The Americans were outnumbered, but ready to do battle.

One can imagine the panic felt by the residents of New Orleans. What to do? Like all people of faith, they prayed. Throughout the night before the battle, the Ursuline nuns, along with many New Orleanians, gathered in the convent's chapel and prayed before the statue of Our Lady of Prompt Succor, praying for the Virgin Mary's intercession.

On the morning of the battle, a statue of Our Lady of Prompt Succor was placed on the altar of the chapel and the Very Reverend William Dubourg, Vicar General, offered a mass in plea for victory. Mother St. Marie Olivier de Vezin, Prioress of the convent, vowed to have a mass of Thanksgiving sung should the Americans be victorious in the battle. It is said that at the "very moment of communion," a courier came into the chapel to inform all those present that General Jackson had won the battle. General Jackson personally thanked the nuns for their prayers, *"By the blessing of heaven, directing the valor of the troops under my command, one of the most brilliant victories in the annals of war was obtained."*

Our Lady of Prompt Succor
statue at Ursulines Convent.

Washington Artillery Park
Decatur Street, across from Jackson Square
Erected: 1976

Washington Artillery Park honors the local 141st Field Artillery of the Louisiana National Guard. The guard has seen action in conflicts since the Civil War.

Looking to the north, Artillery Park overlooks Jackson Square. Here visitors can see the iconic view of the St. Louis Cathedral and Clark Mills' equestrian statue of Andrew Jackson. The southern view from the park is one of the most spectacular views of the Mississippi River. Facing the river and to the right one can see the Crescent City Connection bridge that connects the east and west banks of the city. To the left is the river's famed crescent. The park itself features a model of an 1861 Parrott Rifle used in the Civil War.

Historical Marker #1:

This cannon (model 1861 Parrott Rifle) honors the men of the Battalion Washington Artillery, a Louisiana National Guard unit formed in New Orleans in 1838 as the Washington Artillery Company. It is one of the four Parrott Rifles originally purchased by the unit in 1875 from the Washington Arsenal, and is owned by the Louisiana Historical Association's Memorial Hall, located on Camp St. This site became Washington Artillery Park after Major-General Allison Owen and others rescued a façade fragment from the group's old armory during its demolition and moved it here in 1938 "as a permanent memorial to cannoniers of the old command." In 1972, during park renovations the remnant was demolished."

Historic Marker #2:

On and near this site since 1718 has centered the military activities of both regular and citizen soldiers of France, Spain, the Confederacy and the United States. On either side were the redoubts forming the "Great Battery" which crisscrossed its fires with those of Fort San Carlos (Ft. St. Charles) at the foot of Esplanade Ave. and of Fort San Luis (Ft. St. Louis) at the river end of Canal Street. One block down river is the lot used as an artillery park for Spanish, French and American cannons. From here and from Place Darmer across the street the cannoniers, bombardiers of France, the Royal Artillery of Spain, the Battalion d'Artillerie d'Orleans, and for the last 100 years, the Washington Artillery (141st Field Artillery) have fired the salutes welcoming distinguished visitors to the Crescent City. To them and to their worthy successors this park is dedicated.

Spanish American War
Loyola Avenue @ Poydras St.
Erected: 1939

The New Orleans monument to the Spanish American War veterans stands at the corner of Poydras St. and Loyola Avenue in the CBD.

The artist of the statue is unknown, but it is believed to be designed by, or based on the design of, Theo Alice Ruggles Kitsner's series of statues called "Hikers" to commemorate the Spanish American War veterans in the U.S.

Dedicated in 1939, it originally stood on Canal St. at S. Claiborne St. It honors American soldiers who fought in the Spanish American War. It was later moved to its present location.

Monument Inscription:

> *Erected by the State of Louisiana in honor of her sons*
> *who served in the army and navy in the war with Spain,*
> *the Philippine insurrection and the China Relief expedition*
> *1898-1902. Dedicated May 30, 1939.*

Blue Star By-Way Marker
City Park, Roosevelt Mall
Erected: 2002

Blue Star Highway markers pay tribute to the U.S. armed forces. The program started in 1945 after World War II.

One such plaque in New Orleans is located by the flag pole on the neutral ground along Roosevelt Mall in City Park. It was erected by the Federated Council of New Orleans Garden Club on April 26, 2002. There are 14 Blue Star Memorial **Highway** markers in the New Orleans metropolitan area. However, there are only two **By-Way** markers in the greater New Orleans area; the other marker is located in Lafreniere Park, in Metairie LA.

World War II Memorial
Jefferson Davis Parkway at Tulane Avenue
Erected: 1946

Dedication marker reads: *In honor of the men and women of the third ward who served in World War II and in the memory of those who made the supreme sacrifice. Sponsored by Banks Social and Carnival Club. Dedicated December 8, 1946.*

40

World War I Victory Arch
Burgundy Street
Erected: 1919

The World War I Victory Arch was erected in Macarty Square in the Ninth Ward in 1919. The Arch is reminiscent of the triumphal arches of the Roman Empire. Created by Weiblen, it is a granite structure over 28-feet high by 21-feet wide by seven inches thick.

There are four bronze plaques on the monument. One plaque lists the names of the men who died, two plaques list the white men who served and one plaque lists the African American men who served.

Inscription across the top of the monument reads:

Erected AD 1919 by the people of this the Ninth Ward in honor of its citizens who were enlisted in combative service and in memory of those who made the supreme sacrifice for the triumph of right over might in the Great World War.

Great War Memorial
City Park Avenue,
East of City Park's Pizzati Gate

The Great War Memorial in City Park celebrates all war veterans. The top of the pillar honors the four branches of the military.

Monument inscription:

"In memory of our comrades who made the supreme sacrifice." "To you from failing hands we throw the torch. Be yours to hold it high."

The second line is from a Flanders Fields poem.

Molly Marine
Canal Street @ Elk Place
Erected: 1943

The first statue of a military woman in the U.S. was erected in 1943 on Canal Street at Elk Place. It is of a woman in a military uniform looking in the sky for enemy planes.

Sculpted by Enrique Alferez, the purpose of the statue, according to the inscription, was to *"Free a marine to fight;"* an attempt to interest women in joining the marines for non-combat duty so that the men could go into battle.

The statue was fashioned in the likeness of former Marine and native New Orleanian, Judy Mosgrove. When it was first erected, the statue was made of granite and marble chips rather than bronze because of rationing during WWII. When the statue was rededicated in 1966 to all female marines who serve, a group of Marines raised money to have the statue coated in bronze and placed on top of a marble pedestal.

Monument Inscription:

"Free a Marine to Fight" Rededicated July 1, 1966 in honor of women marines who serve their country in keeping with the highest traditions of the United States Marine Corps.

Historic Marker #1:

On November 10, 1943, the city of New Orleans dedicated the first United States monument of a woman in service uniform: "Molly Marine." A local recruiter commissioned the statue to help recruit women during World War II. Renowned artist Enrique Alferez, a Mexican immigrant who wanted to be a Marine, donated his services. Due to wartime restrictions, the statue was cast in concrete. In 1998, the Molly Marine Restoration Society was formed by the Marine Corps League, Marine Support Group of New Orleans, and Women Marines Association to restore and preserve Molly in perpetuity. This bronze is a replica of the original which still stands proudly stands in New Orleans. The support and generous contribution of CWO3 Kim T. Adamson (USMCR) and the Marine Corps Heritage Foundation made this possible.

Military Women's Memorial Monument
Elk Place @ Cleveland Ave.
Erected: 1962

Also on Elk Place is the Military Women's Memorial Monument, sponsored by the New Orleans Chapter WAC Veterans Association.

The dedication plaque on the monument reads:

To the honor and glory of all military women who offer their lives in defense of the United States in the cause for peace.

There are four dedication plaques on the monument:

*Women of the US Marine Corps.
Women's Auxiliary Reserve in the
Coast Guard (SPARS).*

*Navy Nurse Corps (NNC), US
Naval Reserve Forces
(Yoemanettes-WWI), Women's
Auxiliary Volunteer Service
(WAVES).
Air Force Nurse Corps (AFNC).
Women's Air Force (WAF). Air
Force Medical Specialist Corp
(AFMSpC)*

*Army Nurse Corpse (ANC).
Women's Army Corps (WAC).
Army Medical Specialists Corps
(AMSC).*

*Erected May 30, 1962 under
sponsorship of New Orleans
Chapter, WAC Veterans
Association (AMSC).*

Louisiana Vietnam Veterans Memorial
Poydras St., Plaza Level,
Louisiana Mercedes Benz Superdome
Erected: 1984

The life-sized bronze statue of four soldiers was dedicated in 1984 as a tribute to Louisiana Vietnam Veterans. The statue, which depicts two soldiers carrying a wounded brother-in-arms, was commissioned by the Vietnam Veterans Leadership Program and created by William Ludwig.

Monument Inscription:

Let every nation know whether it wishes us well or ill, that we shall pay any price, bear any burden, meet any hardship, support any friend, oppose any foe to assure the survival and success of liberty. John F. Kennedy, January 20, 1961

The Poydras St. side of the monument is inscribed:

In honor of the service and sacrifice of Louisiana's Vietnam Veterans who, like their forefathers, answered their nation's call to duty.

Inscribed inside the base of the monument are the names of the 881 Louisiana soldiers killed in Vietnam. On the Plaza railing are 22 bronze plaques, which chronicle the events of the war years, 1954-1976.

Vietnamese and American Veterans of the Vietnam War
201 Basin St. @ Iberville St.
Erected: 1987

A second Vietnam Veterans memorial stands on Basin and Iberville Streets. It is dedicated to the Vietnamese Veterans and the American Veterans of the Vietnam War.

New Orleans has a large population of Vietnamese immigrants. In 1985, the New Orleans City Council agreed to set aside a day to honor soldiers from South Vietnam who fought beside American soldiers during the war. June 16, 1985, was declared "Republic of Vietnam Armed Forces Day."

A low wall and garden surround the 18-foot pyramid of polished granite. It was erected in 1987 and is the first monument erected to honor both Vietnamese and American veterans of the Vietnam War.

Inscribed on the side of the memorial facing south are words in Vietnamese: *"Than Kinh Tri An."* Translation: *"Remember with Deep and Sincere Gratitude."*

On the west facing side of the pyramid is the inscription: *"In memory of the American and Allied Forces who bravely fought and sacrificed during the Vietnam War."*

The north side of the pyramid are those words in Vietnamese: *"Thanh-kinh tri-an nhung chien-si anh-hung qlvnch sa vi-quoc vong-than de boa-ve chinh-nghia tu-do tai Vietnam."*

A final inscription: *"This memorial monument was erected in June 1987 by the Vietnamese Veterans Association New Orleans with the financial support of the American Bank and Trust Co."*

Vietnam Veterans statue at the Superdome.

Music

Armstrong Park/Congo Square
835 Rampart Street

Sculpture depicting Africans dancing the *Bamboula* in Armstrong Park.
The sculpture was created by Adewale S. Adenle.

The celebratory gathering of enslaved African vendors in Congo Square, now known as Armstrong Park, originated in the late 1740s, during the colony's French period. By 1803, Congo Square had become famous for the gatherings of enslaved Africans who drummed, danced, sang and traded on Sunday afternoons. Among the most famous dances were the *Bamboula*, the *Calinda* and the *Congo*. These African cultural expressions gradually developed into Mardi Gras Indian traditions, the second line and eventually, New Orleans jazz and rhythm and blues.

Louis "Satchmo" Armstrong
Armstrong Park
Erected: 1980

Born in New Orleans, Louis "Satchmo" Armstrong became a trumpeter, composer, singer and actor. Considered one of the most influential figures in Jazz, he changed the way people played music. Satchmo is widely recognized as a founding father of Jazz. The larger than life statue in Armstrong Park was created by Elizabeth Catlett. The historic marker reads:

"His trumpet and heart brought everlasting joy to the world, embodying jazz as
"The Pulse of Life."

51

Mahalia Jackson
Armstrong Park
Erected: 2010

A statue of Mahalia Jackson stands in Armstrong Park in front of the theater named in her honor. One of the most influential gospel singers in the world, she was renowned for her work in civil rights. The sculpture, created by Elizabeth Catlett, was dedicated in April 2010. Mahalia Jackson died on January 27, 1972.

Monument Plaque:

> *Mahalia Jackson was born in New Orleans and became known as*
> *"the world's greatest gospel singer."*
> *Her powerful voice introduced Black Gospel music to an*
> *international public. She sang in support of*
> *Dr. Martin Luther King, Jr. and the Civil Rights Movement.*

Charles "Buddy" Bolden
Armstrong Park
Erected: 2010

Charles "Buddy" Bolden is recognized as a key figure in the development of New Orleans style rag-time. A legendary cornet player, he is often credited as the earliest jazz musician and band leader. Buddy was among the first to improvise popular music using the black blues and hymn vocal style on a horn. He is remembered as the "first king of jazz".

Music Legends Park
Bourbon Street

Photo credit: photosounds/shutterstock.com

Antoine "Fats" Domino (left)

New Orleans son, Antoine "Fats" Domino was born in the New Orleans' Ninth Ward, the youngest of eight children. His music career began in 1949 and since then he has had 25 gold singles and sold over 65 million records. He is the recipient of the Grammy Lifetime Achievement Award and is a Rock and Roll Hall of Fame Inductee.

Al Hirt (photo center)

Alois Maxwell "Al" Hirt is a local trumpeter and band leader. He began playing his trumpet at the age of six. Over the course of his career, Al played with various swing bands including Tommy Dorsey, Jimmy Dorsey, and Benny Goodman. He also received 21 Grammy nominations. Al died in 1999.

Pete Fountain (photo right)

Jazz clarinetist, Pete Fountain, had a long and successful career. He was a regular on the Lawrence Welk show and appeared on the Tonight Show with Johnny Carson. He owned a club on Bourbon Street and founded the Half-Fast Walking Club in 1960, a regular feature on the streets of New Orleans on Mardi Gras day. Pete died in 2016.

Other Notable Persons

John James Audubon
Audubon Park
Erected: 1910

John James Audubon, renowned ornithologist, naturalist and painter lived in New Orleans for a time. It was here that he started to work on his famed *"The Birds of America"* illustrations.

He came to New Orleans with his family in the early 1820s on a journey to study and paint birds. While in New Orleans, he made a living painting portraits and teaching drawing.

A bronze statue of Audubon, created by Edward Virginius Valentine, stands at the entrance to Audubon Zoo in uptown New Orleans.

Reverend Avery Alexander
University Medical Center
N. Galvez St. @ Canal Street
Erected: 2015

Avery Alexander was a Louisiana civil rights leader and politician, serving in the Louisiana House of Representatives from 1975 until his death in 1999. He marched with Martin Luther King, Jr., participated in voter registration drives and helped to stage a successful boycott of Dryades St. businesses that refused to hire blacks for managerial positions.

In 1963, during a civil rights sit-in at a New Orleans' segregated lunch counter near City Hall, Reverend Avery Alexander was carried out by police officers. Today, a statue of Reverend Avery Alexander stands near the entrance of the University Medical Center. The statue was created by sculptor Sheleen P. Jones.

St. Frances Xavier Cabrini
6300 Canal Blvd. @ Harrison
Erected: 1949

Frances Xavier Cabrini founded the Institute of the Missionary Sisters of the Sacred Heart of Jesus in 1880. She arrived in New Orleans in 1892 and, with the help of a wealthy Italian benefactor, she set to work helping immigrant children orphaned by yellow fever.

She opened her first orphanage on St. Phillip St. in the French Quarter. In 1905, she built the Sacred Heart Orphan Asylum at 3400 Esplanade Avenue. In 1959, that institution became Cabrini High School for girls. She was beatified by Pope Pius XI in 1938 and canonized by Pope Pius XII in 1946.

Winston Churchill
Foot of Poydras Street
across from the Hilton Hotel.
Erected: 1977

At British Place, a triangle of land located across from the Hilton Hotel on Poydras Street, is a statue of Sir Winston Churchill. The statue honoring Churchill was donated to the City of New Orleans by the Partners of International Rivercenter, Coleman Development Company, Hilton Hotel Corporation and Lester Kabacoff, General Partners in 1977.

58

Gayarré Place
2279 Esplanade Ave., Tremé
Erected: 1884

This monument, entitled *Peace, the Genius of History,* was originally displayed at the 1884 New Orleans World's Industrial and Cotton Centennial Exposition by a terracotta company to showcase their material at the expo. When the exposition closed, the monument was purchased by New Orleanian, George Dunbar who relocated it to its present location and dedicated it to Charles Gayarré, noted historian and author of a four-volume Louisiana History, written in early 19th century.

John McKeithen
Louisiana Superdome, Plaza Level, Poydras St.
Erected: 2002

John McKeithen served two terms as governor of Louisiana. He is widely recognized for his work to attract business and industry to Louisiana. He supported the construction of the Super-dome for the new NFL franchise, the New Orleans Saints, saying, *"That could be the greatest building in the world."*

The nine-foot statue of McKeithen was created by Patrick Miller and dedicated in 2002. It stands on the Plaza Level of the Superdome.

Margaret Gaffney Haughery
Margaret Place, Camp and Prytania Streets
Erected: 1884

Margaret Haughery was an Irish woman who devoted herself to doing good works and helping orphaned children. Even as she grieved the loss of every member of her family, she began a dairy and baking company giving most of her earnings to the poor.

When she died in 1882, she left an estate of $30,000 to charity. The money was used to open St. Theresa's Orphanage on Camp St.

The statue of Margaret was created by Alexander Doyle and unveiled July 9, 1884. The monument inscription reads:

She was a mother to the motherless;
she was a friend to those who had no friends;
she had wisdom greater than schools can teach;
we will not let her memory go from us.

Edward D. White, Jr.
400 Royal St.
Erected: 1926

Edward D. White, Jr., born near Thibodaux, was the son of former Louisiana governor, Edward D. White, Sr. He was elected to the state senate in 1874 and served on the Louisiana Supreme Court from 1878 to 1880. He was elected to the U.S. Senate in 1890. In 1894, President Grover Cleveland nominated him to the Supreme Court where he served for 16 years. President William Taft nominated him for Chief Justice in 1910 and he served as such until his death in 1921.

He is best known for formulating the Rule for Reason, which is the standard in anti-trust law. He also sided with Supreme Court majority decision in Plessy v. Ferguson (1896), upholding the legality of separate but equal.

Artist Bryant Baker created the bronze statue of White that stands in front of the Louisiana Supreme Court Building.

Martin Luther King
Felicity and South Claiborne Streets
Erected: 1981

In 1957, American Baptist minister and Civil Rights advocate, Martin Luther King, Jr. met with other southern ministers at the New Zion Baptist Church on LaSalle St and incorporated the Southern Christian Leadership Conference (SCLC).

SCLC is an organization whose goal is to redeem the "soul of America" through non-violent protest. Its mission statement reads: *"In the spirit of Dr. Martin Luther King, Jr., the SCLC is renewing its commitment to bring about the promise of 'one nation, under God, indivisible,' together with the commitment to activate the strength to love within the community of humankind."*

A life-sized bronze bust of Dr. Martin Luther King, created by artist Nancy Johnson, stands on Felicity and S. Claiborne Streets in memorial to the civil rights activist who gave his life for his belief in the equality of all people. Monument inscription: *"I have a dream"*

Don Bernardo de Galvez
Foot of Canal Street
Erected: 1977

In 1777, Spanish military leader Don Bernardo de Galvez became governor of Spanish Louisiana replacing Luis de Unzaga y Amezaga. He is best known for his leadership of the Louisiana militia against the British during the American Revolution.

As governor, Galvez enforced Spain's anti-smuggling laws against the British. He also championed legislation that allowed Louisiana to continue to trade with France and its colonies. In addition, he encouraged immigration to Louisiana. He is specifically known for settling many immigrants from the Canary Islands in Louisiana.

The equestrian statue of Galvez stands at the foot of Canal Street, next to the Canal St. ferry landing. The statue, a gift from Spain, was created by Juan de Avalos is 15-feet tall. It was dedicated in 1977.

Sophie Bell Wright
Magazine Street and Sophie Wright Place.
Erected: 1988

Sophie Bell Wright was a woman filled with compassion and the desire to teach. She started several free schools and the city's Home for Incurables, a care facility for disabled and gravely ill patients. She was an advocate for prison reform and of public playgrounds.

A statue of Sophie stands in uptown New Orleans at the corner of Sophie Wright Place and Magazine Street. The statue erected in 1988 was created by Enrique Alferez.

Alexander Pierre Tureaud
AP Tureaud and St. Bernard Avenue at N. Roman St.
Erected: 1997

A native of New Orleans, Alexander P. Tureaud was the lawyer for the New Orleans Chapter of the NAACP in the 1960s. He successfully argued in McKelpin v. the Board of Education for black teachers to receive the same salary as white teachers. He was also instrumental in fighting to desegregate LSU, New Orleans schools, buses, parks and restaurants.

A bronze statue, made by sculptor Sheleen P Jones, stands in AP Tureaud Civil Rights Memorial Park in New Orleans' Seventh Ward.

deLesseps "Chep" Morrison
Duncan Plaza, Loyola Ave.

Before becoming the city's 54th mayor, deLesseps Morrison was elected to the Louisiana House of Representatives. During World War II, he joined the U.S. Army where he achieved the rank of colonel and received the Bronze Star. In 1944, he was re-elected to the legislature *in absentia.*

Morrison was elected mayor of New Orleans in 1946 where he addressed veterans' housing needs and engaged in urban renewal. He created the New Orleans Recreation Department (NORD) and widened Basin St. where he created the Garden of the Americas, lining the street with statues of prominent Latin American figures.

In 1961, President John F. Kennedy appointed him U.S. ambassador to the Organization of American States. Morrison was killed along with his son and five other people when their plane went down on an international mission in 1964.

The deLesseps Morrison monument in Duncan Plaza was built by the State of Louisiana along with Kaiser Aluminum. It was created by Lin Emory.

George Washington
Orleans Parish Library, Loyola Ave
Erected: 1960

A statue depicting George Washington as a Master Mason stands at the Orleans Parish Public Library on Loyola Avenue near Duncan Plaza. The statue was created by Donald De Lue.

Allison "Big Chief Tootie" Montana
Armstrong Park
Erected: 2010

The Mardi Gras Indian tradition dates to a time when escaped slaves were hunted down. Runaway slaves would often take refuge with American Indian tribes in the area. The Mardi Gras Indian tradition is a tribute to those American Indian tribes for their assistance.

Big Chief Tootie Montana is the great grandson of the Becate Batiste, the first Creole to mask with the Indians. Batiste was the founder of the Creole Wild West, the first Mardi Gras Indian tribe (1880). Tootie Montana served as "Big Chief" of the Yellow Pocahontas Tribe for over 50 years and is revered by all Mardi Gras Indian tribes in New Orleans. He is responsible for turning the culture of the Mardi Gras Indians from one of violence into one of pageantry.

Plaque reads:

Yellow Pocahontas Mardi Gras Indian Tribe/"Chief of Chiefs". A New Orleans cultural icon and internationally recognized master craftsman in the building trade, Big Chief Montana masked as a Mardi Gras Indian for over 50 years. He died in the city council chambers defending the Mardi Gras Indian tradition.

The statue of "Big Chief Tootie" Montana was created by Sheleen Jones-Adenle and stands in Armstrong Park.

Tomb of the Unknown Slave
St. Augustine Catholic Church in Tremé
1210 Governor Nichols
Erected: 2004

At St. Augustine Catholic Church in Tremé is a poignant memorial made of chains and shackles in the shape of a cross that honors the slaves who died and were buried in unmarked graves.

Plaque reads:

On this October 30, 2004, we, the faith community of St. Augustine Catholic Church, dedicate this shrine consisting of grave crosses, chains and shackles to the memory of the nameless, faceless, turfless Africans who met an untimely death in Faubourg Tremé. The tomb of the unknown slave is commemorated here in this garden plot of St. Augustine Church, the only parish in the United States whose free people of color bought two outer rows of pews exclusively for slaves to use for worship. This St. Augustine/Tremé shrine honors all slaves buried throughout the United States and those slaves in particular who lie beneath the ground of Tremé in unmarked, unknown graves. There is no doubt that the campus of St. Augustine Church sits astride the blood, sweat and tears and some of the mortal remains of unknown slaves who either met with fatal treachery and were therefore buried quickly and secretly, or were buried hastily and at random because of yellow fever and other plaques. Even now, some Tremé locals have childhood memories of salvage/restoration workers unearthing various human bones, sometimes in concentrated areas such as wells, in other words, the tomb of the unknown Slave is a constant reminder that we are walking on holy ground, thus we cannot consecrate this tomb because it is already consecrated by many slaves' inglorious deaths bereft of any acknowledgement, dignity or respect, but ultimately glorious by their blood, sweat, tears, faith, prayers and deep worship of our creator.
Donated by Sylvia Barker of the Danny Barker Estate.

Piazza d'Italia
377 Poydras St.
Established: 1978

Italians immigrated to New Orleans as early as the French colonial period. Their numbers increased significantly after Italy's civil war in 1860. Many were uneducated and unskilled and became laborers for the sugar plantations of Louisiana, public improvements and railroad construction. They lived primarily in the Vieux Carré, and worked in distribution, and the sale of citrus fruit. Their business interests later extended to wine, liquor, and truck farming.

The Piazza d'Italia was designed by architect Charles Moore in 1978 and commemorates the Italian heritage of New Orleans.

Across from the Piazza d'Italia is the American Italian Renaissance Foundation Museum & Library on the corner of Tchoupitoulas and Poydras Streets.

Irish Memorial
New Basin Park
Erected: 1990

The New Basin Canal was a shipping channel constructed by the New Orleans Canal and Banking Company from Lake Pontchartrain into the American section of the city. It cost a total cost of $4 million and countless lives.

Construction began on the canal in 1832. There was no heavy machinery at that time to dig the canal, so laborers were needed to dig it by hand. Slaves were considered too valuable to use for this endeavor, so Irish immigrants were hired. Using hand tools, they dug the canal from Lake Pontchartrain, through the swamps of the Metairie Ridge to the site of the old Union Passenger Terminal. The Irish laborers died in great numbers. Death

69

estimates range from 4,000 to 30,000. The exact number is unknown as no one kept track.

The canal was closed after WWI and is now covered by I-10/Pontchartrain Expressway.

On November 4, 1990, the Irish Cultural Society of New Orleans erected a Celtic cross made from Kilkenny marble on the neutral ground at West End Boulevard and Robert E. Lee Blvd. to memorialize the ultimate contributions made by Irish immigrants.

Lafayette Square
Established: 1788

LAFAYETTE SQUARE

Planned in 1788 as a public place for Faubourg Ste. Marie, the City's first suburb, this Square honors American Revolutionary War Hero, Marie Joseph Paul Yves, Roch Gilbert Du Motier, Marquis de Lafayette. He declined the invitation to become the first Governor when the United States purchased Louisiana. During his April 9-15, 1825, visit to the City of New Orleans, his popularity was evidenced by resounding cheers of "Vive Lafayette, Vive Lafayette!"

Originally named Place Gravier, this park was designed in 1788 by Charles Laveau Trudeau, Surveyor General of Louisiana under the Spanish regime. It became the central square for the English-speaking Americans living in New Orleans at the time, much as the Place D'Armes was the gathering place for French speaking Creoles.

The park was renamed for the Marquis de Lafayette in 1824 and is the second oldest public park in New Orleans.

Historic marker:

Planned in 1788 as a public place for Faubourg Ste. Marie, the city's first suburb, this Square honors American Revolutionary War Hero, Marie Joseph Paul Yves, Roch Gilbert Du Motier, Marquis de Lafayette. He declined the invitation to become the first Governor when the United States purchased Louisiana. During his April 9-15, 1825 visit to the City of New Orleans, his popularity was evidenced by resounding cheers of "Vive Lafayette. Vive Lafayette!"

Lafayette Square is the home of several of New Orleans' monuments.

Benjamin Franklin
Camp Street side of Lafayette Square
Erected: 1926

The statue of Benjamin Franklin that stands in Lafayette Square today is the second statue of the American statesman to stand in the Square.

In the early 1900s the first statue of Franklin began to show signs of deterioration from the weather and was moved to the public library in 1909.

The present statue was a gift from a winter resident of New Orleans who often visited the statue. Henry Wadsworth Gustine of Chicago gifted the present statue to replace the first. This statue of Benjamin Franklin, created by Hiram Powers, was erected in 1872. It is a replica of the statue in Chicago's Lincoln Park.

The statue's pedestal, donated by New Orleans Typothetae – a printers' association – honors Franklin's impact on the printing trade.

Henry Clay
Lafayette Square
Erected: 1863

A second American statesman memorialized in stone in Lafayette Square is Henry Clay, Kentucky General Assemblyman and U.S. Senator. Clay narrowly lost the presidential election in 1845. He was a frequent visitor of the city.

71

The Clay monument, sculpted by Joel T. Hart in 1863, was originally located on Canal Street and St. Charles Avenue. It was to be one of a series of statues to line Canal Street, but Clay's monument was the only one erected. In 1900, the city moved the statue to its present location to make way for streetcars and increasing automobile traffic.

John McDonogh
Lafayette Square
Erected: 1898

John McDonogh was born the son of a wealthy Baltimore bricklayer. He moved to New Orleans in 1800 and became a shipping merchant and west bank plantation owner. Even though he owned slaves, he was considered an abolitionist and he devised an innovative way his slaves could buy their freedom over 15 years.

When McDonogh died in 1850, he left half of his estate to the city of New Orleans for the creation of public schools. His bequest to the city, $704,440 (about $18 million today), was tied up in the courts until 1861 when the City Council made the first payment from the McDonogh Fund.

The statue that stands in Lafayette Square was sculpted by Atillio Piccirilli and was paid for with donations from schoolchildren.

A second statue of McDonogh (left) now stands in Duncan Plaza between the Loyola Ave. entrance and Gravier St. Created by Angela Gregory, the sculpture was moved from Lafayette Square in May 1977.

José Martí
Jefferson Davis Parkway
Erected: 1996

José Martí was a Cuban patriot who supported his country's liberation from Spanish colonialism in the 1800s. His statue, erected by Liceo Cubano José Martí and Club Cubano de Profesionals, was a gathering place for members of the Cuban community who left Cuba before 1959.

Plaque (translated from Spanish):

From the Cuban exiles and their friends in Louisiana to the city of New Orleans, at the closing of the centennial year of his death fighting for the liberation of Cuba. New Orleans 28 January 1996.

Garden of the Americas
Basin Street @ Canal Street
Erected: 1957

Through the 19th and 20th centuries, New Orleans was a center of trading between the United States and Latin America and earned a reputation as a gateway to the Americas.

The "Garden of the Americas" was conceived by Mayor Morrison as part of a city-wide beautification project in 1957, as a symbol of friendship between New Orleans and Latin America. The Garden of the Americas covers the neutral ground on Basin St. It contains statues of Benito Juárez, Simon Bolivar and General Francisco Morazán.

Simón Bolívar
Basin @ Canal Streets
Erected: 1957

Called "The Liberator" because he led campaigns that freed several Latin American countries from the Spanish empire at the end of the 18th century, Simón Bolívar symbolizes justice and freedom from oppression.

The neutral ground where the monument stands was once the site of the Southern Railroad Terminal, designed by Daniel Burnham in 1908. The terminal was demolished in 1956 in preparation for the monument.

The monument, which is 12 feet high and made of granite, was sculpted by Venezuelan sculptor Abel Vallmitjana. At one time the memorial included a fountain and reflective pool, but today those aspects of the memorial are merely worn and dirty stone and steel. The bronze emblems representing Venezuela, Columbia, Ecuador, Peru, Bolivia and Panama, once resting in the stone walls of the garden, have been removed, but the statue still stands tall and proud.

Benito Juárez
Basin and Conti Streets
Erected: 1972

Benito Juárez is credited for modernizing the Republic of Mexico. He was exiled twice from his country, finding refuge in New Orleans both times. He resided for a while on St. Peter St. where he earned money rolling cigarettes and cigars at a tobacco factory before reclaiming his presidency in 1861.

This monument was given to the city by Mexico in thanks for sheltering Juárez. The statue resides in the neighborhood where Juarez lived while in exile.

Sculpted by Juan Fernando Olaguibel, the statue was dedicated May 17, 1972 on the 100th year anniversary of Juárez's death.

General Francisco Morazán
Basin St. @ St. Louis St.
Erected: 1966

Francisco Morazán is considered the most important military leader in Central American history. He was a member of the Central American Liberal Party and was President of Federal Republic of Central America. He was Head of State of Honduras, Guatemala, El Salvador and Costa Rica. Morazán is recognized for his attempts to transform Central America into a large and progressive nation.

The statue was a gift of the people of Honduras and Republic of El Salvador in recognition of New Orleans as gateway to the Americas.

The bronze statue, which stands on a five-sided brick and concrete base with granite panels, was created by Mario Zamora. It was dedicated October 21, 1966.

Death and Funerals
Cities of the Dead

As we've seen in earlier chapters, New Orleans' cemeteries have a number of monuments built by military benevolent organizations in honor of a person or organization. But it's not just the military for whom monuments are erected. Families incorporate statues on ordinary graves and vaults, as well.

Firemen Charitable Association
Greenwood Cemetery
Erected 1887

Notable Events

Rebirth
Louisiana Superdome
Erected: 2012

"Rebirth" is a bronze statue depicting New Orleans Saints player, Steve Gleason, blocking a punt by then Atlanta Falcons' player, Michael Koenen, on September 25, 2006, during Monday night football.

The monument was commissioned by Tom Benson, owner of the New Orleans Saints, as a tribute to Gleason's lifetime accomplishment and to the reopening of the Dome after the destruction caused by Hurricane Katrina and the subsequent flooding caused by the federal levee breaches. The sculptor of the monument is Brian Hanlon. *"The statue is symbolic of the Rebirth of our city, our region, our home, our team."* Tom Benson.

Mardi Gras Fountain
Lakefront
Installed: 1962

The Mardi Gras Fountain, dedicated on September 16, 1962, celebrates the city's *laissez les bon temps rouler* lifestyle and love of Carnival. It is the brain child of local Mardi Gras entrepreneur, Blaine Kern.

Designed by Harry Grimball of Favrot and Grimball Architects, it was built at a cost of $42,000. The design featured dancing sprays of water colored by lights of purple, green and gold and surrounded by 80 ceramic tile plaques displaying the crests of the carnival krewes.

The fountain underwent a $2.5 million renovation and repair in May 2005, to repair damaged plumbing, replace damaged tiles and to add tiles for krewes established since 1962. Unfortunately, Hurricane Katrina damaged the newly renovated fountain in August of that year.

In September 2013, with the help of $1.3 million from FEMA and the work of the Army Corps of Engineers, the Levee District refurbished the fountain.

Katrina Memorial
5056 Canal Street
Erected: 2008

In the Charity Hospital Cemetery is the memorial to more than 1500 people who died during Hurricane Katrina and subsequent flooding from the federal levee breaches.

The memorial consists of six mausoleum-like structures that surround the commemorative stone that symbolizes the eye of the storm. Beneath the structure lie 80 unclaimed and unidentified bodies of Katrina casualties. These people were buried with ceremony as part of the memorial dedication.

The Katrina Memorial was dedicated August 29, 2008, three years after Hurricane Katrina devastated the Gulf Coast.

Katrina Scrap House
Convention Center Blvd.
Erected: 2009

Artist Sally Heller unveiled her memorial of Hurricane Katrina on August 29, 2009, on Convention Center Blvd. across from the Ernest N. Morial Convention Center where thousands of refugees sheltered after the storm until help arrived.

The art depicts a battered house in a tree, broken windows, crooked porch and Mardi Gras beads hanging from the roofline.

81

ELEVEN
700 Elysian Fields
Erected: 2016

Deepwater Horizon was a deep water offshore drilling rig owned by Transocean and leased to BP Oil from 2001 through September 2013.

On April 20, 2010, while drilling at the Macondo Prospect in the Gulf of Mexico, a blowout caused an explosion causing the death of 11 crewmen and the largest oil spill in U.S. The explosion and subsequent oil spill wreaked havoc in the waters of the Gulf of Mexico and on the lives of thousands of people who made their living in those waters. Beaches from Texas to Florida were affected by the spill as were wetlands, marine and wild life.

ELEVEN is a memorial to the 11 crewmen who died in the explosion. It consists of 11 life-sized human figures. The memorial was conceived by Michael Manjarras of Sculpture for New Orleans and created by Mississippi artist Jason Kemes.

Miscellaneous

The city of New Orleans is a living museum and everywhere you turn there are historical plaques and markers memorializing events and people of its past.

French Quarter

1. **Archbishop Antoine Blanc Memorial** – 1112 Chartres St. On the grounds of the Old Ursuline Convent.
2. **Birthplace of Danny Barker** – 1027 Chartres St. – African American Creole guitar and banjo player. Jazz Hall of Fame member. Recipient of National Endowment of the Arts Music Master Award.
3. **Bosque House** – 619 Chartres St. Built in 1895 by Bartholome Bosque of Palma, Majorca. Between 1777 and 1785 this was the site of the home of Don Bernardo de Galvez, Spanish Governor of Louisiana. It was here on Good Friday, March 21, 1788 that a disastrous fire began, which destroyed most of the city.
4. **David Bannister Morgan** – 617 St. Peter St. "The Flanking Battery" Battle of New Orleans.
5. **Edgar Degas House** – 307 Exchange Pl. This house was bequeathed to Degas and his sister by their maternal uncle Michael Musson.
6. **Faulkner House** – 624 Pirate Alley. Where Faulkner wrote his Nobel prize winning novel, "Soldier's Pay."
7. Former site of the **Holy Family Sisters' Convent** – 715 Orleans St.
8. **French Market** – 1008 N. Peters Street. Traditional market where Native Americans traded in ancient times and locals still operates today.
9. **Jackson Square** – Chartres St. at Place John Paul II.
10. **Judge Fred J. Cassibry Square** – 440 Royal St. Cassibry was a US Navy WWII veteran, served on N.O. City Council, Orleans District Court, US District Court, E.D. La and the Louisiana Economic Development and Gaming Board.
11. **Literary Landmark** – 540 St. Peter St. Residence of Sherwood Anderson, author of "Winesburg, Ohio."
12. **Louis J. Dufilho, La Pharmacie Francaise**, 514 Chartres St.
13. **Maison Hospitalière** – 1220 Dauphine St. Non-sectarian nursing home. Established in 1893 by La Société des Dames Hospitalières.
14. **Jack Teagarden** – 428 Bourbon St. The last place where Teagarden played in 1964.
15. **Indian Portage** – Decatur St., south of St. Ann.
16. **Old Ursuline Convent** — 1112 Chartres St.
17. **Original Old Absinthe Bar** – 240 Bourbon St., Established 1806
18. **Original Pierre Maspero's Slave Exchange** – Established 1788.

19. **Pat O'Brien's** – 720 St. Peter Street. Built in 1791 as private home that became first Spanish Theater.
20. **Pierre Maspero's Exchange** – 540 St. Peter St. – Where defenses of New Orleans were planned 1814-15.
21. **Quartier General de la Garde Municipale** – 616 Pirates Alley.
22. **Residence of Don Manuel Lanzos**, Capt. of the Spanish Army, 628 Dumaine St. Now Madam John's Legacy.
23. **Shangarai Chasset** – Gates of Mercy – North Rampart St between Conti and St. Louis Streets. Site of first permanent Jewish house of worship in state of Louisiana.
24. **Site of First Louisiana School**, 1725 – 625 St. Ann Street.
25. **Site of First U.S. District Court** – 919 Royal Street.
26. **Site of Kolly Townhouse, First Ursuline Convent and Charity Hospital** – 301 Chartres St.
27. **U.S. Branch Bank** – 301 Chartres Street – First residence of Ursulines nuns in 1727
28. **U.S. Mint** – 420 Esplanade Ave.
29. **Pontalba Buildings** – Upper and Lower – Jackson Square
30. Birthplace of "Dixie" – 140 Royal Street. Citizens State Bank stood on this site from 1835-1924. They were the originator of the "Dixie" $10 bank note.
31. Site of the **French Opera House** – 541 Bourbon Street.
32. The **Steamer New Orleans** – Across the street from Jackson Square. The steamer *New Orleans* first arrived at this spot in 1812.

Down River from French Quarter

1. **Civil Rights Pioneers/History** – 5909 St. Claude Avenue. Site of the integration of Southern Elementary School November 14, 1960
2. **Fort St. Charles** – 400 Esplanade Avenue at North Peters Street. Where the executions were of French patriots in the Louisiana Rebellion of 1768.
3. In **Memory of All American Veterans** – 3421 Esplanade Avenue in St. Louis Cemetery III. Memorial honoring all American veterans.
4. **Italian Hall** – 1020 Esplanade Avenue. Unione Italiana, Italian benevolent societies.
5. **Edgar Germain Hilaire Degas** – 2306 Esplanade Ave. French Impressionist master whose mother and grandmother were born in New Orleans.
6. **Faubourg Marigny** – 449 Esplanade Avenue. First suburb of the original city.

7. **Faubourg Tremé** – Esplanade Ave and N. Claiborne Ave – Morand-Moreau plantation subdivided into what is considered to be America's oldest existing African American neighborhood.
8. **Solomon Northup** "12 Years a Slave" – Esplanade Ave. near Chartres Street. – Site of Theophilus Freeman's slave pen.
9. **The Historic Lower Ninth** Ward/Industrial Canal Flood Wall – Intersection of Jourdan Ave and N. Johnston St.
10. **Plessy v. Ferguson**, Press St. Railroad Yards – Intersection of Press and Royal Streets. Site of Homer Plessy's arrest.

Uptown

1. **Audubon Room** – 402 Dauphine St. The Creole cottage is considered the site of the studio of John J. Audubon when he lived in New Orleans.
2. **Brevard-Rice House** – 1239 First St. Built in 1857 for Albert Hamilton Brevard. 1869-1935 owned by Emory Clapp family; 1935-1947 owned by family of Dr. Frank Brostrom; 1947-1972 owned by Judge John Minor Wisdom; 1972-1988 owned by John A. Mmahat. Purchased in 1989 by novelist Ann Rice and her husband, poet and painter, Stan Rice.
3. **DeDroit Residence** – 735 Henry Clay Ave. Home of John "Johnny" DeDroit was a cornetist and bandleader.
4. **Gilbert Academy and New Orleans University** – 5318 St. Charles Ave. Black educational institutions conducted by the Methodist Church 1873-1949.
5. **Jefferson Davis** - 1134 First Street. President C.S.A.
6. **Mayor Isaac W. Patton House** – 1527 Washington Ave.
7. **National Shrine of Our Lady of Prompt Succor** – 2701 State St.
8. **R.N. Girling's "English Apothecary"** – 2726 Prytania St.
9. **Van Benthuysen-Elms Mansion** – 3029 St. Charles Ave. Built in 1969 for "Yankee in Grey," Capt. Watson Van Benthuysen, II, CSA.
10. Starting point of the first traditional New Orleans Mardi Gras Parade – Intersection of Julia and Magazine Sts.

Central Business District/Downtown

1. **Canal Street Historic District** – Canal Street is the widest thoroughfare with a broad neutral ground, the traditional dividing line between the Creole and American sectors of the city.
2. **The Clarinet & Jazz** – 330 Loyola Avenue. This neighborhood is considered one of the original birthplaces of Jazz.

3. **Touro Infirmary** – 1174 Convention Center Blvd. Original site of Touro Infirmary built by Judah Touro in 1852.
4. **U.S. Customhouse** – 423 Canal St.

Warehouse District

1. 8-inch **Columbaid Cannon Marker** – Camp St. near Andrew Higgins Dr. Cast of Alabama iron by the Confederates at Selma, AL in Spanish Fort, Mobile Bay. The cannon now resides in front of the Louisiana Civil War Museum at Confederate Memorial Hall, 929 Camp Street.
2. **Atlantic Wall Fragments** – 945 Magazine St. Three slabs of steel reinforced concrete that ran from the Franco-Spanish border in the south to Norway. The "Atlantic Wall" was the bunker that housed the German artillery and machinery.
3. **Higgins Boat** (LCVP) – St. Charles Ave. and Felicity St. Site of Higgins Industries, designers America's first successful tank landing craft.

MidCity

1. **17th Street Canal Floodwall** – Bellaire Dr. at Stafford Pl. *On August 29, 2005, a federal floodwall atop a levee on the 17th Street Canal, the largest and most important drainage canal for the city, gave way here causing flooding that killed hundreds."*
2. **Charity Hospital Cemetery** – 5056 Canal St.
3. **Heinemann Park/Pelican Stadium** – 4002 South Carrollton Ave. Home of New Orleans' first professional sports team, the New Orleans Pelicans baseball team.
4. **Marvin E. Thames** – 615 City Park Ave. Director of Isaac Delgado Trade Schools 1954-1958; Dean and President of Delgado Trades and Technical Institute 1958-1962; President of Delgado Community College 1962-1979
5. **Pitot House**, 1440 Moss St. Home of first mayor of incorporated New Orleans.

New Orleans East/Lakeview

1. **Fort Pike** – 5 miles west on U.S. 90.
2. **London Avenue Canal Floodwall Breach** – 4902 Warrington Dr.

City Park

1. **Monteleone Pillars** – 1914. Two 25-foot marble pillars at the entrance to the park in front of NOMA, erected in memory of Anthony Monteleone, former park commissioner.
2. **Dueling Oak** – Dueling was a popular way to settle disagreements in the city. This oak is the remaining dueling oak along City Park Ave. The second Dueling Oak was lost in the 1949 hurricane.
3. **Popp Bandstand** – Bandstand designed by Architect Emile Weile. Inscribed on the frieze.
4. **Gragard Memorial** – 1918. Decorated marine killed in action in a battle near Bouresches, Aisne, France. Plaque located on Victory Avenue close to the Pavilion of Two Sisters.
5. **Cox Memorial** – 1918. Walter Cox killed July 9, 1918; Wallace Cox, died July 28, 1918. Memorial plaque located between Victory Ave and the Botanical Garden exit.
6. **Bradburn Memorial** - 1918. In memorial of Donald Bradburn who fought in St. Mihiele and Meuse-Argonne offenses in France. Died October 1918. Plaque located close to the sidewalk on Victory Ave. close to the Pavilion of Two Sisters.
7. **Hyams Fountain** – 1921. Outside gates to Carousel Gardens. Dedicated to the Children of New Orleans.
8. **Dreyfous Bridge** – 1924. In memory of by Mr. and Mrs. Felix J. Dreyfous who donated the Dreyfous Ave. bridge to City Park. This bridge replaced the original wooden bridge. Felix Dreyfous was N.O. citizen who tended City Park in its infancy.
9. **Anseman Bridge** – 1928 – In memory of Victor Anseman, "father of City Park." The current bridge replaced original built in 1938 by the WPA. Crosses Bayou Metairie.
10. **Popp Fountain**–1934. Reportedly, Popp and Isabel Grant donated $25,000 for a memorial fountain. Other sources report Rebecca Grant donated funds for a fountain as a memorial to Rebecca and John Popp and that Mrs. Grant requested that it be designed by the Olmsted brothers. The central waterspout was designed by Enrique Alferez, WPA artist.
11. **Tad Gormley** – 1935/36. Originally known as City Park Stadium, renamed Tad Gormely after his death in 1965. Francis Thomas "Tad" Gormley was athletic director for City Park in 1938.
12. **Peristyle** – 1935. Peristyle was designed as a venue for dancing by architect Paul Andry in 1906. Originally called the Peristyleum. Flanked by four large concrete lions created by Pietro Ghiloni. Renovated in 1930s and in 1989.

13. **McFadden Girl Scout Cabin** – 1936. Donated to City Park by William Harding McFadden.
14. **FDR/Roosevelt Mall** Eagle Posts – 1936-37 – On Roosevelt Mall. Named after President Franklin D. Roosevelt in memorial of his support of the park. Two posts were relocated in 2016 and relocated to The Helis Foundation Enrique Alferez Sculpture Garden.
15. **Grandjean Bridge** – 1938. Bridge crosses the bayou behind NOMA. Memorial to former park commissioner George H. Grandjean who designed the original lagoons.
16. **Storyland** – 1956. Dedicated to the Children of New Orleans in memory of Mr. and Mrs. John W. Batt. Storybook-themed playground located near the historic Carousel House.
17. **Fort St. John (Spanish Fort)** – 1959. Located on Bayou St. John near the intersection of Jay St. and Beauregard Ave. near the Lakefront. Site of former defense fort and amusement park/resort.
18. **Metairie and Gentilly Ridges Historical Marker** – 1964. Marker stands at Carrollton Avenue and Moss St. along Bayou St. John. It was the first highway through the city, extending from what is now the City of Kenner to Chef Menteur.
19. **Allard Plantation Marker** – 1968. Carrollton Ave and City Park Ave along Bayou St. John. The Allard Plantation was purchased by his grandfather in 1770s. John McDonogh acquired the plantation in 1845 and gave it to the city in 1850.
20. **Colony Grove Marker** – 1976. Daughters of the American Revolution provided trees native to the original 13 colonies for the establishment of a Bicentennial Memorial Garden near the McDonogh Oak. Plaque located near City Park Ave. and Solomon Place. Unfortunately, few trees remain.
21. **The Beatles** – 1984. Commemorates the 20th anniversary of the 1964 Beatles concert in Tad Gormley Stadium. Plaque located inside the Marconi Dr. entrance.
22. **Carousel** Historic Place Designation – 1988. "The Flying Horses." The oldest ride in City Park, it dates back to 1906. Historic horses were restored in the 1980s and in 1988, 2006 (after Hurricane Katrina) and 2015.
23. **Timken Center** – 2000. Timken Center was named after Henry H. Timken. The building is also known as the Casino Building. Henry Timken was one of the founders of the Louisiana Land and Exploration Co. He acquired Couba Island in 1920 and donated the Island to the park in 1996 in honor of his family.

24. **Pizzati Gate** – 2001. The originally called the Alexander Street
    entrance, the gate is located on City Park Ave. and Anseman Ave.
    Steamboat Captain Salvadore Pizzati donated the archway in 1910.
25. **Colombier de Carol** – 1928. City Park Pigeonierre, designed by Felix
    Dreyfous and given to the park in 1928. Located on Pigeon Island near
    the Casino Building.
26. **Stanley Ray Playground** – The Stanley Ray Trust funded the
    playground along Dreyfous Avenue, named the Stanley Ray
    Playground. A statue of Stanley Ray was erected within City Putt.

www.ingramcontent.com/pod-product-compliance
Lightning Source LLC
Chambersburg PA
CBHW071948100426

42736CB00042B/2364